Native Americans

Kiowa

Barbara A. Gray-Kanatiiosh

ABDO Publishing Company

visit us at
www.abdopublishing.com

Published by ABDO Publishing Company, 4940 Viking Drive, Edina, Minnesota 55435. Copyright © 2007 by Abdo Consulting Group, Inc. International copyrights reserved in all countries. No part of this book may be reproduced in any form without written permission from the publisher. The Checkerboard Library™ is a trademark and logo of ABDO Publishing Company.

Printed in the United States.

Cover Photo: © Lindsay Hebberd/Corbis
Interior Photos: AP/WideWorld p. 29; Corbis pp. 29, 30; Getty Images p. 4
Illustrations: David Kanietakeron Fadden pp. 7, 9, 11, 13, 15, 17, 19, 21, 23, 25, 27
Editors: Rochelle Baltzer, Megan M. Gunderson
Art Direction & Maps: Neil Klinepier

Library of Congress Cataloging-in-Publication Data

Gray-Kanatiiosh, Barbara A., 1963-
   Kiowa / Barbara A. Gray-Kanatiiosh.
      p. cm. -- (Native Americans)
   Includes bibliographical references and index.
   ISBN-10 1-59197-654-5
   ISBN-13 978-1-59197-654-7
   1. Kiowa Indians--History--Juvenile literature. 2. Kiowa Indians--Social life and customs--Juvenile literature.
   I. Title. II. Native Americans (Edina, Minn.)

E99.K5G73 2006
978.004'97492--dc22

                                                                        2005049308

About the Author: Barbara A. Gray-Kanatiiosh, JD
Barbara Gray-Kanatiiosh, JD, Ph.D. ABD, is an Akwesasne Mohawk. She resides at the Mohawk Nation and is of the Wolf Clan. She has a Juris Doctorate from Arizona State University, where she was one of the first recipients of ASU's special certificate in Indian Law. Barbara's Ph.D. is in Justice Studies at ASU. She is currently working on her dissertation, which concerns the impacts of environmental injustice on indigenous culture. Barbara works hard to educate children about Native Americans through her writing and Web site, where children may ask questions and receive a written response about the Haudenosaunee culture. The Web site is: www.peace4turtleisland.org

About the Illustrator: David Kanietakeron Fadden
David Kanietakeron Fadden is a member of the Akwesasne Mohawk Wolf Clan. His work has appeared in publications such as *Akwesasne Notes*, *Indian Time*, and the *Northeast Indian Quarterly*. Examples of his work have also appeared in various publications of the Six Nations Indian Museum in Onchiota, NY. His work has also appeared in "How the West Was Lost: Always the Enemy," produced by Gannett Production, which appeared on the Discovery Channel. David's work has been exhibited in Albany, NY; the Lake Placid Center for the Arts; Centre Strathearn in Montreal, Quebec; North Country Community College in Saranac Lake, NY; Paul Smith's College in Paul Smiths, NY; and at the Unison Arts & Learning Center in New Paltz, NY.

Contents

Where They Lived

The Kiowa (KEYE-uh-waw) called themselves *K'uato*, which means "pulling out." This name comes from a creation story. According to the story, the first Kiowa people were pulled out of a hollow cottonwood log. Their Comanche neighbors called them *Kaigwa*.

The Kiowa homelands were originally located in present-day western Montana. Over time, the Kiowa **migrated** southeast to the Great Plains. There, Kiowa territory consisted of parts of present-day Kansas, Oklahoma, and Texas. Neighboring tribes included the Arapaho, Osage, Apache, and Comanche.

A variety of landforms were found on Kiowa territory. Rolling hills covered some areas, and flatlands and grassy plains filled other parts. There were also canyons, valleys, and mountains. And lakes, rivers, and marshes spread throughout the land.

Buffalo roamed the plains on Kiowa homelands.

4

Kiowa territory was home to many plants and animals. There were thick forests, shrubs, berry bushes, and colorful wildflowers. Buffalo and prairie chickens were often found on the grassy plains. And birds such as ducks, quail, and geese lived on Kiowa homelands.

Kiowa Homelands

5

Society

The Kiowa often moved to follow **migrating** buffalo herds and ripening wild plants. As they traveled, they formed small bands. Each band consisted of 12 to 48 tepees. These created a small village.

Kiowa society was organized into four class levels. The highest level included warriors, chiefs, and priests. Subchiefs, medicine men, and property owners were in the second level. The third level consisted of poor people. And, those who did not fit in or were mentally ill were part of the lowest level.

Class levels were changeable. People could move up a level by earning an honor. But if they misbehaved, they could fall to a lower level.

Warrior societies were another important part of Kiowa social structure. The Kiowa had six warrior societies, which were based on age and experience. The *Polanyup*, or Rabbit Society, was the first society. All young boys could join this society to learn basic warfare skills.

The *Ka-itsenko*, or Dog Warriors, was a society of special men. Kiowa men belonged to the *Ka-itsenko* after having a vision or a dream about a dog. They were respected leaders and protectors. Another special group was the *Koitsenko*. To be named a member of this group was the greatest Kiowa military honor. Only the ten bravest warriors could be in the *Koitsenko* at any time.

Kiowa families lived in tepees and traveled with others in their band to search for food.

Food

The Kiowa hunted and gathered. The men hunted small animals such as rabbits, prairie dogs, geese, quail, and ducks. They used traps or bows and arrows to catch them. They used spears, knives, or bows and arrows to hunt larger animals. These animals included buffalo, elks, pronghorn, and deer.

Kiowa men had to work hard to hunt buffalo. Sometimes they wore wolf hides. This disguise let them get close enough to the buffalo to kill it.

Other times, groups of hunters chased large animals off cliffs or into enclosures. Cliff falls often killed or severely injured the animals. And, animals trapped in an enclosure were easier to kill.

While Kiowa men hunted, the women gathered wild fruits and vegetables, seeds, roots, and nuts. They brought these foods back to their villages to prepare for their families. They used meats and vegetables to cook soups and stews. And, they dried extra food to eat during cold weather. The women made a mixture called pemmican from dried buffalo meat, **tallow**, and berries. The Kiowa often ate pemmican while traveling.

The Kiowa felt that it was important to make use of the entire buffalo. They used the hide to make clothing, saddles, robes, and bedding. They boiled the hooves to make glue. And they carved the horns into spoons, bowls, and cups.

It was common for a Kiowa man to wear a wolf hide when hunting buffalo.

Homes

The Kiowa lived in tepees. Each tepee housed a family of four or five people. A large tepee was about 20 feet (6 m) in **diameter**. It was about 20 feet (6 m) tall.

The women were in charge of constructing tepees. Setting up and taking down tepees was a quick process because the Kiowa moved so often. First, the women erected three wooden poles to form a triangle. Then, they added more poles to build the frame.

To make the tepee cover, the women sewed buffalo hides together with **sinew**. Then, they wrapped the cover around the tepee frame and fastened it at the front with wooden pins. Finally, the women pounded stakes through the bottom of the cover and into the ground. This made the tepee stable.

At the bottom of the tepee, the women left an opening for an entrance. This was usually 36 to 48 inches (91 to 122 cm) high and always faced eastward. A flap made from hide covered the entrance.

In the center of the tepee, the Kiowa kept a fire burning for warmth and for cooking. Smoke escaped through the top of the tepee. There were beds along the walls. The Kiowa built the beds from willow rods and covered them with buffalo hides.

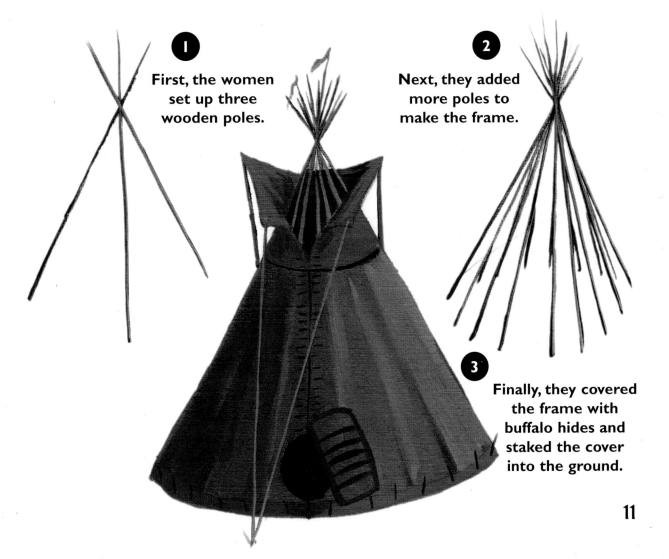

1 First, the women set up three wooden poles.

2 Next, they added more poles to make the frame.

3 Finally, they covered the frame with buffalo hides and staked the cover into the ground.

Clothing

The Kiowa wore clothing made from elk, deer, and buffalo hides. The women used shells, porcupine quills, and animal bones to decorate the clothing.

The men wore **breechcloths**, shirts, and hip-length leggings. The leggings protected their legs from brush and thorns. The women wore leggings and long dresses. The dresses were fringed along the bottom and around the arm openings.

Both men and women wore moccasins. The moccasins had a flap that dragged on the ground. As it dragged, it left a special track. The flap was decorated with **quillwork** or beadwork.

In cold weather, the Kiowa wore buffalo robes. They used hides from buffalo taken in the fall, when their coats are thickest. The hair side of the robe was worn touching the body. This trapped in heat. The Kiowa often painted or embroidered their robes.

The Kiowa parted their hair in the middle. Sometimes, the women wore their hair in braids. The men wore their hair in long braids wrapped with strips of fur. They also wore part of their hair short over the right ear. This was a symbol of their tribe.

Kiowa women decorated their dresses with elk teeth. The teeth were thought to have powerful love magic.

Crafts

The Kiowa were skilled at crafts. They painted tepee covers, animal hides, and containers for storage. They used paint made from mixtures of dirt, clay, and rocks. And, they used paintbrushes made from long buffalo hairs.

The women painted straight lines, circles, and triangles on containers made from **untanned** hides. The Kiowa used these containers to store food, tools, quills, and sacred items.

The men painted tepee covers. Families sometimes owned tepee designs, which were passed on from father to son. Others came from a dream or a vision. The painters believed these designs protected those living inside the tepee.

Painters also recorded historical events on buffalo hides. Each hide contained the events that happened during a time span of about six months. The pictures often included Kiowa villages, sun dance ceremonies, and warriors on horseback.

In the 1920s, a group of Kiowa men were recognized for their artistic talent. After studying at Oklahoma University, they became known as the Kiowa Five. Their names were Spencer Asah, James Auchiah, Jack Hokeah, Stephen Mopope, and Monroe Tsatoke. They preserved Kiowa painting styles and became a positive influence for Native American artists.

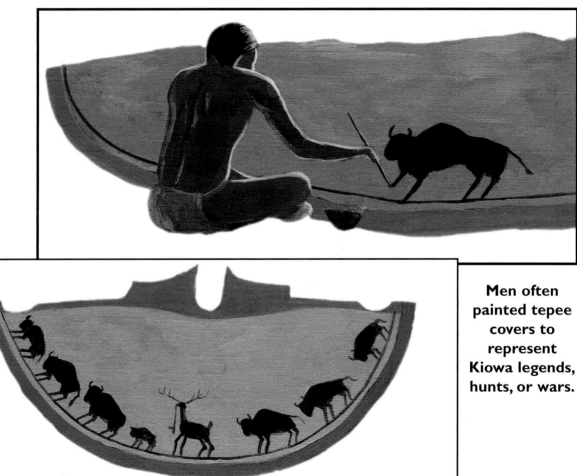

Men often painted tepee covers to represent Kiowa legends, hunts, or wars.

15

Family

When a Kiowa man wanted to marry, he gave a horse to the woman's parents. If the gift was accepted, a marriage contract was made. Then, the couple usually lived with the woman's parents.

Kiowa villages contained **extended families**. Each person was expected to contribute to the survival of the band. Typically, roles and responsibilities depended on gender and age.

Kiowa villages depended on skilled hunters to bring back food. So, a man's most important job was hunting. Men used natural materials to make hunting tools. They carved wood to make bows and arrows. And, they used flint and **obsidian** to make arrowheads. They attached the arrowheads to the arrows with **sinew**.

The women prepared hides for making tepee covers and clothing. First, they stretched them out and staked them into the ground. Then, they scraped away the remaining meat and hair.

Next, they **tanned** the hides to make them soft enough to use. Finally, the women sewed them together. To do this, they used **awls**, thread made from **sinew**, and needles made from bone.

Kiowa women worked together to scrape animal hides and prepare them for use.

Children

Kiowa children learned many useful things from listening to the elders. They also learned by helping with daily tasks in their villages. The men taught the boys how to make weapons, hunt, and protect their villages.

The women taught the girls how to prepare, cook, and dry foods. Girls also learned how to prepare and sew hides. It was their responsibility to care for younger children, too. And, Kiowa girls learned the art of tepee construction.

In their free time, Kiowa children played games. One of their favorite games was played on ice using a slider and a bone. The slider was about five inches (13 cm) long and carved from a buffalo rib. It had two long wooden pegs that added another 12 inches (30 cm) to the slider. The object of the game was to slide the bone the farthest.

The Kiowa used dogs to carry children when they traveled. To do this, they attached a **travois** to a dog. The travois was

A-shaped, and the larger end dragged behind the dog. It was made from short, wooden tepee poles. They also used this device to carry the elderly or ill people.

Later, the Kiowa used horses to pull **travois** because horses could manage heavier loads. Kiowa children became skilled horse riders at a young age.

Kiowa children were often pulled on a travois when families traveled.

Myths

The Kiowa pass myths on from generation to generation to teach people about life. The following is a Kiowa myth about how the world became light.

Long ago, people on this side of the world lived in darkness. One day Fox, Deer, Magpie, and Saynday discussed this problem. "On the other side of the world, a sun gives off light and makes things grow," Saynday said.

"Maybe we could bring the sun here somehow," Deer suggested. Together, they made a plan. Fox could run the farthest and the fastest, so he left to find the people who kept the sun.

When Fox arrived at their village, the people were playing a game. He watched as they rolled the sun on the ground like a ball. Fox had a sneaky idea. He joined the game, ran off with the sun, and brought it back to his village.

At first, Saynday and the others were happy. But soon, there was too much light. Darkness never came, and the plants overgrew. Saynday decided to throw the sun into the sky. Then, it gave light to both sides of the world.

According to this story, Saynday threw the sun into the sky to share the light with the whole world.

21

War

The Kiowa used several types of weapons during battles. Warriors fought with bows and arrows, knives, spears, and **tomahawks**. Knives and spear points were made from flint or **obsidian**. Early tomahawks were made from wood and stone. Later, they were made from metal. The Kiowa used many of these weapons as hunting tools, too.

Warriors wore strong armor to protect themselves during battle. The armor prevented arrows, knives, and spears from piercing the skin. They wore breastplates and chokers made of beads carved from buffalo bone or horn. They also carried painted shields made from **untanned** buffalo hides.

Spanish explorers brought horses to Kiowa territory in the early 1700s. This changed traditional Kiowa warfare styles. The Kiowa shortened their bows so they were easier to use while fighting on horseback.

The Kiowa became expert horse riders. Horses enabled them to travel farther. And horses became an important part of hunting and trading. Soon, they became a symbol of power and wealth. They were even a common form of payment.

Kiowa warriors painted designs on their shields that were often inspired by a vision or a dream.

Contact with Europeans

During the late 1700s, the Kiowa traded with the French and the British. They traded horses and other goods for guns, metals, and vermilion. Vermilion was a bright red substance the Kiowa used for face paint.

Western expansion in the United States brought many new settlers to Kiowa territory. The large groups of people scared away the animals and killed the plants. The Kiowa had a hard time finding food and supplies. So around 1790, the Kiowa and the Comanche joined forces to fight the new settlers.

In 1867, the United States sought peace with the Kiowa, Comanche, Cheyenne, and Arapaho. The federal government persuaded the tribes to give their land to the United States. In exchange, it promised the tribes secure **reservations**.

Later that year, the Kiowa were among several Native American tribes to sign the Medicine Lodge Treaty. The treaty established a combined reservation for the Kiowa and Comanche in present-day southwest Oklahoma. It promised the tribes many things, including clothing, doctors, and schools. The treaty could not be altered except by a vote from the tribes.

However, fighting continued. Later, the federal government realized there had been miscommunication. Some of the tribe leaders who signed the treaty had not fully understood it.

Representatives of the federal government encouraged the Kiowa and other Native American tribes to sign the Medicine Lodge Treaty.

Lone Wolf

There were many famous Kiowa leaders. Some felt that peace with the United States was the best way to protect the people. Others felt that resistance was the best solution.

Lone Wolf was a famous Kiowa chief who believed in the power of resistance. He led the Kiowa as they fought for their land. Lone Wolf refused to sign the Medicine Lodge Treaty. He did not trust the federal government to keep its promises.

After the treaty was signed, Lone Wolf encouraged the Kiowa to resist the federal government's orders. Many Kiowa refused to live on their assigned **reservation**. So in 1868, General Philip Henry Sheridan held Lone Wolf and another Kiowa resistance leader named Satanta **hostage**. Lone Wolf and Satanta would be released when the Kiowa moved to their reservation.

Eventually, Lone Wolf was released. After that, he participated in the Red River War against the Texas Rangers in 1874. But, the loss of men and horses was too destructive. Lone Wolf became depressed and surrendered in 1875. The federal government thought imprisoning Lone Wolf would help to end tribal resistance. So, he was arrested. While in prison, he contracted malaria. Lone Wolf died in 1879, soon after his release from prison.

Lone Wolf led the Kiowa in resisting the U.S. government.

# The Kiowa Today

In the late 1800s and early 1900s, the United States passed laws to **assimilate** Native Americans. These laws were designed to help Native Americans adopt the European **culture**. One of the many laws forced children to be sent away to boarding schools. There, they were educated in European ways.

The Kiowa continued to fight for their land and rights. In 1892, a group of people wanted a portion of Kiowa land set aside by the Medicine Lodge Treaty. The federal government allowed this without getting the agreed-upon vote. So in 1903, the Kiowa brought their concerns to the U.S. Supreme Court. The Kiowa argued that the federal government had made promises it hadn't kept. But, the Kiowa lost the case and had to give even more land to new settlers.

Currently, the Kiowa and the Kiowa-Apache are both **federally recognized** tribes. Both tribes have federal trust lands in southwest Oklahoma. Today there are about 12,242 people who are full or part Kiowa.

The Kiowa still maintain their cultural traditions. It is important that children learn tribal customs to pass on to future generations. Many children take Kiowan language classes. And, the Kiowa participate in sacred dances at powwows.

Right: Kiowa novelist and professor N. Scott Momaday won the 1969 Pulitzer Prize for Fiction for his novel House Made of Dawn.

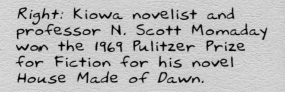

Left:
Kiowa artist Vanessa Jennings stands in front of her grandfather's artwork. She is the granddaughter of Stephen Mopope of the Kiowa Five.

The Kiowa gather for the
Kiowa Black Leggings Ritual
Powwow on Veterans Day
weekend. This sacred
celebration honors Native
American veterans. Above,
Kiowa girls watch as the
adults perform a traditional
dance. To the right, a boy
and his father wear black
leggings and red capes.
Veterans display their military
medals on the capes.

Glossary

assimilate - to become a comfortable part of a new culture or society.

awl - a pointed tool for making small holes in materials such as leather or wood.

breechcloth - a piece of hide or cloth, usually worn by men, that wraps between the legs and ties with a belt around the waist.

culture - the customs, arts, and tools of a nation or people at a certain time.

diameter - the distance across the middle of a circle.

extended family - a family that includes grandparents, uncles, aunts, and cousins in addition to a mother, father, and children.

federal recognition - the U.S. government's recognition of a tribe as being an independent nation. The tribe is then eligible for special funding and for protection of its reservation lands.

hostage - a person held captive by another person or group in order to make a deal with authorities.

migrate - to move from one place to another, often to find food.

obsidian - a hard, glassy rock formed when lava cools.

quillwork - the use of porcupine quills to make designs on clothing or cradleboards.

reservation - a piece of land set aside by the government for Native Americans to live on.

sinew - a band of tough fibers that joins a muscle to a bone.

tallow - the melted fat of cattle and sheep.

tan - to make a hide into leather by soaking it in a special liquid.

tomahawk - a light ax used for throwing and as a hand weapon.

travois - a type of vehicle used to transport loads. It consisted of a frame of two wooden poles tied together over the back of an animal and allowed to drag on the ground.

Web Sites

To learn more about the Kiowa, visit ABDO Publishing Company on the World Wide Web at **www.abdopub.com**. Web sites about the Kiowa are featured on our Book Links page. These links are routinely monitored and updated to provide the most current information available.

31

Index